Guru Nanak
and a Disciple's Family Attachments:
Our Attachments Keep Us in the Cycle of Life and Death

Adapted from a story told by Sant Ram Singh Ji on January 14, 2016 and January 6, 2017

Illustrated by Carlos Brito

"It is our desires that make us unhappy."   Sant Ram Singh Ji

Guru Nanak and a Disciple's Family Attachments

Guru Nanak and a Disciple's Family Attachments: Our Attachments Keep Us in the Cycle of Life and Death is a story originally told in a Satsang by Sant Ram Singh Ji on January 14, 2016 and January 6, 2017 during Meditation Retreat Programs at RadhaSwami Ashram, Channasandra Village, Karnataka, India.

Special thanks to those who critiqued and reviewed the story:
Kathryn Boulet, Graham Leavett-Brown,
Richard Malarich.
Their suggestions have made the adult story more appropriate for children.

Translated by Ashok Shinkar
Transcribed by Ali Czernin, Geoff Halstead, & Harvey Rosenberg

Once again, Carlos Brito has used color and characters to make this story book a delightful visual journey for children and adults. Thank you, Carlos, for your exceptional work that makes our hearts dance with joy.

DISCLAIMER: There are a few scenes in the story book that might be too violent for young children. Yet, the message in the story is so important that we deemed it worthy of publication. However, we suggest you preview the entire story book before allowing children to read it on their own. Thank you.

ISBN-13: 978-1-942937-16-6

(c) 2017 All Rights Reserved

Published by
Go Jolly Books
www.gojollybooks.com
74 Gem Ln., Sandpoint, ID 83864

FIRST EDITION, GO JOLLY BOOKS, First Printing
2017
10 9 8 7 6 5 4 3 2 1 Printed in the U.S.A.

Guru Nanak
and a Disciple's Family Attachments:
Our Attachments Keep Us in the Cycle of Life and Death

Adapted from a story told by Sant Ram Singh Ji on January 14, 2016 and January 6, 2017

GO JOLLY
BOOKS

INTRODUCTION

In January, 2014, at RadhaSwami Ashram, Channasandra Village, Karnataka, India I asked Sant Ram Singh Ji if I could take stories He told in Satsang and publish them as books.

Although I don't recall His exact words, He said yes. Then, He told me to make sure the books were for children. I took this to mean I could substitute words more suitable for children. With His Limitless Grace, reviewers of the first four books have told us we have made the books easier for children to understand.

Guru Nanak and a Disciple's Family Attachments: Our Attachments Keep Us in the Cycle of Life and Death shows how a devotee's attachments bring suffering to him. The disciple spends no time in devotion and focuses completely on his worldly desires. Yet, Guru Nanak ultimately showers His Grace and liberates the disciple.

It's a beautiful story that shows us the importance of where we place our attention on a day to day basis. The illustrations are vibrant and fun. Whimsical color combinations and characters truly make the story come alive. We hope you enjoy it.

DISCLAIMER: There are a few scenes in the story book that might be too violent for young children. Yet, the message in the story is so important that we deemed it worthy of publication. However, we suggest you preview the entire story book before allowing children to read it on their own. Thank you.

Radhaswami,
Harvey Rosenberg

Guru Nanak
and a Disciple's Family Attachments:
Our Attachments Keep Us in the Cycle of Life and Death

Dedication

This book is dedicated to Sant Ram Singh Ji,
a Sant Mat Master Who has Limitless Grace,
Unconditional Love and Acceptance of us.
He attempts to make us like Himself and is a True Friend.

During Guru Nanak Ji's time, there was a disciple who had taken initiation. He spent no time in devotion to his Master and lived his whole life in worldly pursuits. Even in his dreams he did not remember his Master. He was very attached to his family, his farm work and his animals, especially cattle.

Because of his attachment to his animals, when the man died, he was reborn as a calf. He was well looked after and played a lot during his first three years. He felt really loved. Then, the family began to train him for farming by attaching him to a plow.

During the training, family members sometimes had to beat the calf so he could learn to obey what he was being asked to do. The family members didn't know any other way to train the calf, and they didn't know he was their father in the previous life.

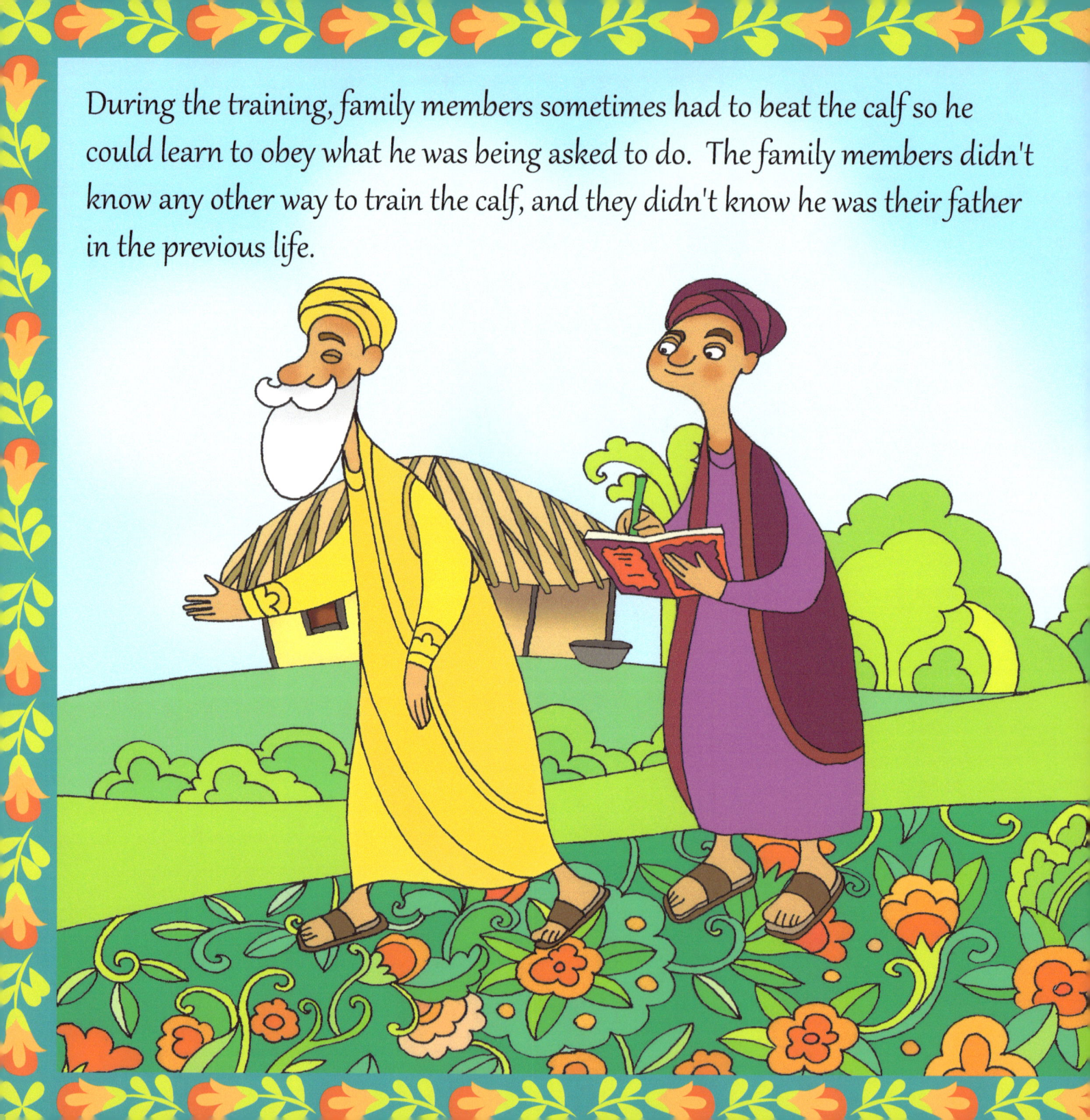

Guru Nanak Ji was nearby with Mardana. Guru Nanak was reciting a Bani and Mardana was writing it down. Suddenly, Guru Nanak started laughing.

Mardana asked Him why He was laughing, as there was nothing in the Bani that was funny.

Nanak Ji stated, "This jiva, who was with me, was to rise above the human form, but instead, he has gone into lower forms and is now born as a bullock."

Mardana replied, "He must be suffering a lot and maybe now he's ready to listen to the Teachings. Why don't we try to bring him on the Path?"

Guru Nanak Ji agreed with Mardana and so They went to the family where the bullock was. The family greeted Nanak Ji and Mardana warmly, gave Them a good meal, then asked Them what had brought Them there.

Nanak Ji told them, "I want to see one of your bullocks."

When Guru Nanak Ji saw the bullocks, He went to the bullock whose soul was initiated by Him. Guru Nanak caressed the bullock and then whispered in the bullock's ear, "Are you ready to come with me now?"

But the bullock replied, "One of the other bullocks I work with is weak. Because I am strong, I make up for his weakness. If I go with you, the family won't be able to farm properly and will suffer. I need to stay here to help with the farming."

Saints do not use force to make Their initiates do something. Guru Nanak, seeing him attached as a bullock and still lost in being attached to his previous family, left him there.

Bullocks normally live for eighteen years, but when they are made to work very hard, they don't live that long. After a few years, the bullock's soul left the body when the bullock died.

But, because the man was still attached to the family and had strong desires there, he was reborn again in the same place. This time, however, as a dog in his old family. He felt loved and was happy to be there.

Nearby, Guru Nanak Ji and Mardana were sitting below a tree, when Mardana asked about the initiate who was a bullock. Nanak Ji replied he had died and was reborn as a dog.

Mardana felt sad to hear this. Again, he requested Nanak Ji to shower His Grace on that poor soul, who may be suffering as a dog and might be ready to accept the Path.

Guru Nanak Ji said, "He is my initiate, so let's go see if he's ready now."

They again went to the family, which was a well-to-do family, who greeted Them warmly. Guru Nanak Ji mentioned He had come to see their dog. Saints are able to communicate with the soul, They know the language of the soul, so when Nanak Ji was massaging the dog, He asked, "Are you at least ready to come now?"

The dog replied, "These people leave their door open, they don't take care of the house and if a thief comes, he can steal anything from the house."

Since Saints never impose anything, Nanak Ji and Mardana walked away from there.

One day, the initiate's daughter-in-law was preparing millet rotis and was cooking one roti over the fire. She needed water, and when she went to fetch some, she left the roti on the stove.

The smell of the roti cooking was so delicious that the dog rushed inside and pulled that roti out of the pan and started eating it.

When the lady returned, she saw the dog eating her roti and completely forgot that she loved this dog. Her mind caused her to be so angry and upset that her face became mean and cruel.

She set the pot of water aside, grabbed a stick, and waited angrily at the door.

She was so furious that her love for the dog disappeared. When the dog ran, she hit him so hard that she broke his backbone. She didn't know this dog was her father-in-law in his previous life, which might have stopped her from striking the dog.

Because there was no one to care for the dog, he stayed outdoors near the house, suffered a lot and within a month and a half, he died, still attached to the family.

So, again he was reborn in the same place, this time as a snake. He was very attached to his grandchildren and would go to see them. The family members would see the snake and try to catch him, but he hid from them.

One day, when all the family members were cutting grass at their farm, the granddaughter was crying at home in her bed.

It was painful for the snake to hear his granddaughter crying, so he left his hiding place and went to comfort and soothe her. He began playing with her and the granddaughter became quiet.

However, one of the family ladies returned to fetch water. She saw the snake, who was on the bed with the little girl, and threw the pot of water at the snake. Then she ran to call the girl's parents and told them a snake had bitten their daughter.

Even though the snake was dripping wet, he continued to play with the girl, completely forgetting that he was a snake, and not the girl's grandfather. Four family members came with sticks and beat the snake to death, even though he had done nothing wrong to the girl.

However, even after suffering such horrible treatment from people who once loved him, the man was still attached to the family. He again was reborn, this time as an insect the size of a grain of rice in a gutter of dirty water that went from the house into the backyard.

Nearby, Nanak Ji was giving a discourse and Mardana Ji was writing it down when Mardana inquired, "What ever happened to that devotee who was born as a bullock?"

Nanak Ji told him, "He died as a bullock. Thereafter, he took the form of a dog, then he died as a dog. After that he became a snake, then in the next life now, he is an insect and lives in a gutter. And after this he will be reborn as a tree near their house."

Mardana became upset hearing about the poor man's miserable lives and prayed, "You must help him, Nanak Ji, because this jiva is so attached, he is not going to come back as a human in this world on his own."

Nanak Ji replied, "You're correct, and I myself am getting old, so let's go and get him now."

They returned to the same house and again were well received. They stated that They needed to use the washroom and went outside behind the house in the back.

There, behind the house, Nanak Ji told Mardana where this insect was. Mardana Ji then used two sticks to remove the insect from the gutter.

As soon as the insect was placed on the ground, Nanak Ji crushed it with His toe. And then with His Grace, He gave him the life of a human being.

So Kabir Sahib says, "The souls spend so much time in worldly pursuits. They don't understand the reality and they don't follow the words of the Masters."